SELF-INITIATION

Secrets of Spiritual Enlightenment

BY MIKE BHANGU

BBP
Copyright 2020

Copyright © 2020 by Mike Bhangu.

This book is licensed and is being offered for your personal enjoyment only. It is prohibited for this book to be re-sold, shared and/or to be given away to other people. If you would like to provide and/or share this book with someone else, please purchase an additional copy. If you did not personally purchase this book for your own personal enjoyment and are reading it, please respect the hard work of this author and purchase a copy for yourself.

All rights reserved. No part of this book may be used or reproduced or transmitted in any manner whatsoever without written permission from the author, except for the inclusion of brief quotations in reviews, articles, and recommendations. Thank you for honoring this.

Published by BB Productions
British Columbia, Canada
thinkingmanmike@gmail.com

TABLE OF CONTENTS

Introduction
The Sacred Frequency
The Supreme Master
The Resurrection
Dead yet Alive
The Second Death
Three Days
Mool Mantra
All is Within
How The Master Answers
Holy Companions
The Four Ages
In the Beginning...

INTRODUCTION

I ask—What's worth knowing and practicing on this esoteric journey and what doesn't serve our higher self? What are the true spiritual teachings able to lift our consciousness to the next level of existence? What are the lessons that will take us closer to ONENESS? What are the secrets of Initiation?

Like a Shakespearean tragedy, tragically, the required knowledge is allusive, and in this epoch, no popular institution is teaching this wisdom. A person must seek this knowledge without knowing where to begin the quest. To make the journey a little more hopeless, the knowledge is locked behind an unknown closed door, 50 feet thick, and guarded by 1000 armed men—metaphorically speaking. The task to learn tangible spiritual truths is Herculean. Yet, this is the duty of every living person. With this understanding, a person might emancipate the self and exist as a being who radiates true love and happiness. Without this awareness, does one truly live?

My name is Mike Bhangu. I've spent over twenty years researching and ten years writing, and I present to you an understanding after scrutinizing the different philosophies, philosophers, religions, mystics, holy texts, and holy individuals.

I commenced my quest to understand my place within this world over two decades back and my first step was taken inside the academic arena. I studied the great thinkers immortalized by the Western World such as Plato, Socrates, Aristotle, Thomas Hobbes, Rene Descartes, Jean-Jacque Rousseau, Karl Marx, John Locke, John Rawls, Niccolò Machiavelli, René Descartes, David Hume, Thomas Aquinas, Marcus Aurelius, Émile Durkheim, Max Weber, Bertrand Russell, Leo Strauss, and so on.

From there I travelled to the East, and with my eyes, I listened to the dead such as Laozi, Mencius, and Confucius.

Then I pried the great minds engulfed by the fringes of academia such as Madame Blavatsky, Manly P. Hall, Francis Bacon, and St. Germaine.

By now I was exhausted, and to add to the privation, my finances grew wings and fled, my social circle shrunk as cotton does in the dryer, and depression was entering and exiting my space at will. Yet questions still rattled about my noggin and I was unable to change direction. So, I tightened the shoelaces, turned my hat to the back, and scrutinized the different theologies and religions.

At the feet of The Infinite I fell and I studied the different holy texts and individuals such as Thoth, Manu, Moses, Guru Nanak,

Guru Gobind, Mohammad, Zoroaster, Buddha, and Jesus. The holy texts examined were *the Gathas, the Gospels, the Qur'an, the Tablets of Thoth, the Book of the Dead, the Old Testament, the Kabbalah, the Zohar, Guru Granth Sahib Ji, Upanishad, Bhagavat Gita*, and a few others.

Over twenty years of searching have passed, and through this manuscript I share with you the core spiritual truths able to move a person closer to ONENESS, and what some seekers call the secrets of Initiation.

The knowledge I present herein is the same truth taught by the great philosophers, mystics, holy texts, holy persons, and the mystery schools of our past. However, for one reason or another, today, these teachings are understood differently than originally intended, and these misunderstandings are now the popular interpretations.

Since the meaning of words and ideas changed and words and ideas are now incorrectly understood, there are many spiritual houses, many interpretations, and many religions instead of one. Yet, all true holy persons, philosophers, and mystics taught the same core truths, and all worked to guide a person toward the three points of the Celestial Triangle.

In addition to explanations able to help you understand this chaotic world and the self, this manuscript will discuss these three points in detail, and according to the Enlightened, if the three are understood, a person will know all he or she requires to know. Moreover, a person acquires the potential to become one with ONE. This is the ultimate state of being. This is true serenity and happiness.

Before I share what the Celestial Triangle truly represents, please receive the words I use with an open mind and without preconceived ideas. I suggest this because the popular interpretations of the three aren't correct, and if unable to relinquish the preconceptions, the notions I share will not resonate.

The three points are God's Spirit (God Manifest), God's Name, and God's Word. This Sacred Trinity unlocks true love, true happiness, and spiritual liberation. But what is God's Spirit, God's Name, and God's Word? In short, they are not what you most likely think they are. Abandon what the popular schools of thought have taught and recognize God's Name and God's Word as a sacred vibration, and God's Spirit as The Manifest aspect of The Source.

God's Spirit is The Supreme Spiritual Master and this Master will never mislead an individual. Moreover, this Master rests within every individual, as with God's Word and God's Name.

The Sacred Trinity is Universal but the Universality of the Trinity might not be apparent since each true philosophy and religion have forgotten. In their amnesia, new or partial associations surfaced. With the older traditions, these interpretations arose soon after the previous epoch ended, near 5000 years ago.

According to the *Mahābhārata*, this era was ushered in by an epic world battle and catastrophic natural disasters. This left behind a planet in chaos. Knowledge was lost. Civilizations were forced to start over again and only partial understanding was retained. Before this epoch, in my opinion, the Celestial Triangle was popularly understood as I explain it.

After pushing aside the popular understandings, The Trinity can be found in most religions, and in short, I've discovered the Celestial Triangle in the following theologies.

In the Egyptian tradition, Osiris represents God's Name, Horus represents God's Word, and Isis represents God's Spirit.

In the Hindu/Vedic house, Shiv represents God's Word, Brahma represents God's Name, and Vishnu represents God's Spirit.

Within the Sikh doctrine, Sat Naam represents God's Name, Shabad represents God's Word, and Sat Guru represents God's Spirit.

In the Christian doctrine these three are represented by Father, Son, and Holy Spirit. The Father represents God's Name. The Son represents God's Word. The Holy Spirit represents God's Spirit. Although Christianity was birthed in this epoch, the early Christians understood the Trinity as above, particularly the Gnostic Christians, but as a result of the European dark ages and the many political incursions, the Celestial Triangle is now understood as something else. And this is true of all religions. Each appears to associate what I present with other aspects and not The Word, The Name, And God's Spirit.

The sacred book of the Mayan Quiches, *Popol-vuh*, suggests that Tzakol, The Supreme Deity, has three aspects: Bitol (the maker), Alom (the engenderer), and Qaholom (he who gives being).

Zoroaster represented the Triad as fire, sun, and light.

The ancient Chinese too respected a Triune God. As suggested by the *Hi-Tse*, The Great Unit, or Y, is three and three are the Great Unit. Yet, the Great Unit has no body or shape. Tao-Tse, in his book, *Tao-te-King*, writes of the Triad:

"That reason, Tao, produced one. That one produced two, that both produced three; and that three had produced all things."

Several ancient philosophers also recognized the Celestial Triangle. For example, Orpheus and Plato represented The Creator/The Demiurgos as Triple—the Three Kings. And the Athenian philosopher, Damascius, celebrated The Infinite as a Thrice Unknown Darkness. Yet, above the Three Kings is The Emperor, The Infinite, known as "Ra" to the Chaldeans. (*Sacred Mysteries, Among the Mayas and the Quiches. 11, 500 Years Ago. By Augustus Le Plongeon, 1886*).

From the Christian tradition we learn that the Trinity is One. From the Egyptian adepts we learn that Isis and Osiris are required for The Word to be. From the Vedic house we learn that the three are able to manifest and take physical form. From the Chinese house we learn that the three produce all things. From the Sikh tradition we learn that without the Trinity, the highest salvation cannot be experienced.

The Word and The Name are specific vibrations / frequencies / sounds. The Word and The Name are within each person but are quasi-dormant and must be awoken or activated. For this to occur, the guidance of God's Spirit is required. All true spiritual philosophies are designed to connect an individual with God's Spirit.

The Trinity, as I present it, in my humble opinion, is the secret of secrets taught by the early mystery schools. Of course, I can't be sure. Their teachings are clandestine and those who know the lessons keep them locked within. I'm guessing an oath of secrecy is involved and loyal they are to that cause.

In my case, I come from the fringes of society and I've gone unnoticed. I've knocked on the door, once or twice, but I must be invisible because society opened the entrance, looked through me, took a few steps outside, glanced left, glanced right, and went back in—closing the door as they did. Don't feel sorry for me. It was a blessing. Independently learning has come with a gift. In my ignorance I'm free to express what others deem secrets, and God's Word, God's Name, and God's Spirit are the keys to all creation. These three must be experienced before a person can unite with The Great Architect and achieve the highest existence, in this life and the next. The following articles explore the Sacred Trinity in more detail.

THE SACRED FREQUENCY

God's Word is a concept missed by many, and again, through no fault to them. Truths are hidden, the person is misdirected, and without understanding the meaning of God's Word, true reality cannot be apprehended.

All popular religions teach that their Holy Book is God's Word and no other book can claim this honour. Each further suggests that the other religions are inferior. Nevertheless, the Holy Books do not associate The Word with the entirety of any Holy Book or religion. In the modern world, God's Word is misunderstood.

To add, the whole of a Holy Book consists of words and not just a single word. In the different books, within this context, when God's Word is described, it isn't pluralized. Yet, religions associate God's Word with words, sentences, and paragraphs.

> *"In the beginning was the Word, and the Word was with God, and the Word was God."* — (John 1:1)

God's Word as a collection of words doesn't truly make sense. I struggled for many years hoping to rationalize the popular depiction taught by the different religions. I couldn't do it.

However, outside the accepted notations, placed within the original context, God's Word is an easily understood phenomenon.

Yes, it's true and the phrase "God's words" is used in some of the Holy Books, yet, this doesn't reference God's Word. In addition, in *the Old Testament* and *the New Testament*, the notion of "God's Word" is applied in different ways and with different means—furthering the confusion. At times, it refers to what God supposedly said to a person, and at other times, it references God's Word as I present it. Moreover, it's evident that meaning was lost in translation and the English versions of the different Holy Books do not give the same messages as those in the original languages. My suspicion is that the original documents are much clearer as to what God's Word truly is.

God's Word isn't the whole of any Holy Book and God's Word is a sacred frequency / sound / vibration.

How did I come to this revelation? By recognizing that there is truth in every true religion and then independently travelling deep into the different religious literature. This said, the Sikh Holy Book, *Sri Guru Granth Sahib Ji*, was instrumental in teaching The Word as a primal vibration and revealing the common celestial thread linking every true religion. *Sri Guru Granth Sahib Ji* explicitly deals with concepts that are hidden in other Holy Texts.

This Holy Book is akin to a key able to decode the other theologies. The Sikh Guru freely reveals what the mystery schools conceal. Without the teachings of the Sikh Guru, it might've taken me several more decades to grasp the concepts I present, if at all.

Unfortunately, the popular notion of The Word, amid the Sikhs, as the others, is also wrongly linked to the entirety of their Holy Book. Sometimes, what is written isn't what's popular.

> *"The Unstruck Sound-current of the Shabad, the Word of God, vibrates in the Court of the Lord."* — (Sri Guru Granth Sahib Ji, ang 1137 of 1430)

> *"When the body dies, where does the soul go? It is absorbed into the untouched, unstruck melody of the Word of the Shabad (God's Word)."*—(Sri Guru Granth Sahib Ji, ang 327 of 1430)

The Word of God is a sacred frequency / sound / vibration. The Word resonates within everything that exists and is responsible for setting the whole of creation in motion. Everything that exists is in a state of vibration, and without this sacred frequency, nothing has a constitution.

> *"...that by the word of God the heavens were of old, and the Earth standing out of the water and in the water."*
> — (2 Peter 3:5)

A theory of Quantum Mechanics, *String Theory*, suggests that extremely tiny string-like particles pervade and vibrate through everything within the Universe. The characteristics of these strings are very similar to the characteristics given to God's Word.

When you read the different Holy Books, without the misdirection, "God's Word" is described as I present it. What's more, The Word understood as a collection of words and sentences doesn't allow the mind to comprehend many doctrinal passages. Take the following as examples. They make little sense under the popular definition but are easily grasped if applied as a sacred vibration.

> *"For the word of God is alive and active. Sharper than any double-edged sword, it penetrates even to dividing soul and spirit, joints and marrow; it judges the thoughts and attitudes of the heart."* — (Hebrews 4:12)

> *"The grass withers and the flowers fall, but the word of our God endures forever."* — (Isaiah 40:8)

The Word is in every person but rests until awoken. When fully active within the body fortress, the person becomes one with "All", and simultaneously inherits the supernatural abilities that accompany the activation. Those as demonstrated by Jesus, Nanak, Moses, Enoch, Buddha, and Hermes Trismegistus (Thoth).

When The Word is awake within a person, a purification of the mind and body pursue. He or she rises above the faults and duality of the body. Herein, the influences of the body no longer communicate to the time and space of thought. As a result, the spirit is released and becomes the dominant source of information influencing a person's thoughts and actions. Since the spirit is the conduit to The Father, in such a state, a person is in harmony with God's Will. The Source flows through him or her. This is what John meant when he wrote, *"The Word became flesh and made his dwelling among us."* (1:14)

The Word, or what Laozi, also known as Lao-Tzu, called "Tao", is unbelievably powerful. When active, the vibration unlocks salvation, unlocks nirvana, and unlocks the all-in-one medicine for every ailment. Moreover, the consciousness expands to incorporate the unconsciousness and the two halves of a person become one—"The higher-self" and "this self" unite, and the invisible and the visible are simultaneously perceivable by a wake mind. It is the meeting of the groom and the bride.

The subtle nature of all that exists is known by those The Word is active within, and through The Word, the subtle nature can be influenced. A change in the subtle translates into a change in the physical nature of a thing, and this is how men as Jesus performed miracles such as healing the sick, walking on water, raising the dead, and multiplying bread. They modified or corrected the blueprint (the subtle) to bring about a physical modification or correction.

Everything in existence was first conceptualized by The Great Architect. Then it manifest as a metaphysical thing—spirit—blueprint. After which, the physical evolved from the subtle. Consequently, all material things exist within the parameters of their subtle essence. The mystics of the world, past and present, can perceive the invisible nature of existence and they're able to influence this essence.

The invisible component to everything that exists occupies the same space as the material. If a mystic desires to manifest matter or influence a material thing, he or she first manipulates the subtle essence. There is a correlation. A change in the subtle effects the physical and vice versa. To manifest matter, the mystic first creates the subtle essence and then the physical naturally comes into existence.

This interpretation of The Word isn't popular and I believe it initially was—particularly, amid the Gnostics. During the very end of writing this article, I was introduced to the 13 books that constitute the *Nag Hammadi Library*. After a brief glimpse, one of the books in this Christian Gnostic collection literally presents The Word as I present it.

Knowledge is power and the most powerful are spiritual truths. God's Word can transform a sheep into a Heavenly lion capable of commanding supernal laws. If a person can comprehend this, *John 14:12* might reveal its vagueness.

> *"Verily, verily, I say unto you, He that believeth in me, the works that I do shall he do also; and greater works than these shall he do; because I go unto my Father."*
> — (John 14:12)

The power of The Word is indescribable and from The Word comes all creation, within all creation is The Word, and in The Word all merge. However, within a person, The Word is silent and must be triggered. For this to occur, assistance is required and only God Spiritually-Manifest can help.

Another idea of utmost importance, communicated by many, many Holy Books, and explicitly by the Sikh Holy Text, *Sri Guru Granth Sahib*, is the value of God's Name.

God's Name, or Sat Naam (True Name), is hidden within all creation, and as The Word, is a sacred vibration. When revealed, it gifts the person with intuitive spiritual wisdom and mystical knowledge. Moreover, The Name is salvation and The Name is nirvana. The Name is so because it activates the unstruck sound current of "The Word" within a person.

> *"Those who are attached to the Naam, the Name of the Lord, are saved; without the Name, they must go to the City of Death. O Nanak, without the Name, they find no peace; they come and go in reincarnation with regrets. ||24||"* — (Sri Guru Granth Sahib Ji, ang 1415)

> *"Whoever obtains the Naam, the Philosopher's Stone, becomes the embodiment of Truth, manifest and radiant throughout the world."* — (Sri Guru Granth Sahib Ji, ang 1392)

The idea of The Name is within most religious doctrine and the vibration that is The Name, as with The Word, supports the constitution of everything that exists. Without this support, nothing, excluding God, can be.

> *"Good deeds, righteousness and Dharmic faith, purification, austere self-discipline, chanting, intense meditation and pilgrimages to sacred shrines - all these abide in the Shabad."* — (Sri Guru Granth Sahib Ji, ang 1332)

> *"Those who die in the Word of the Shabad are saved. Without the Shabad, no one is liberated."* — (Sri Guru Granth Sahib Ji, ang 1416)

As with The Word, The Name is within every person, and as with The Word, God's Name is dormant until awoken and only God reveals God's Name. In specific, God Spiritually-Manifest. God is said to be Unmanifest and Manifest, and the following article explores this notion further.

> *"I am a sacrifice to my True Guru, who has revealed the Lord's hidden Name to me.||2||"* — (Sri Guru Granth Sahib Ji, ang 697)

> *"Without serving the True Guru, the Naam is not obtained. The Naam is the True profit in this world.||6||*

True is His Will, beauteous and pleasing through the Word of the Shabad. The Panch Shabad, the five primal sounds, vibrate and resonate." — (Sri Guru Granth Sahib Ji, ang 1057)

THE SUPREME MASTER

After spending many years examining religions, I was blessed with a revelation, the awareness of God's Spirit.

The person comes into the world innocent, with little knowledge of the reality cast into, and an individual learns of the world from the givers of information such as governments, movies, music, corporations, the family tree, and religions.

Regrettably, all of them have the potential to, purposely or accidentally, communicate inaccurate knowledge and a person can grow to live a life governed by an untruthful value system.

The consciousness can be misinformed and an individual can live a lie without knowing it. But there is a teacher forever truthful and who is eternally incorruptible. This giver of knowledge will never purposely or unknowingly mislead an individual. I forever salute God Manifest.

The idea of God Manifest is in almost all religions and in *the New Testament*, *the Old Testament*, and *the Qur'an* the terms The Spirit, The Holy Spirit, and The Spirit of God signify God Manifest. The Sikh doctrine knows God's Spirit as Sat Guru (True

Guru). Thoth called The Manifest, Primander. The Buddhists know The Spirit as Maitreya.

> *"Therein descend angels and the Spirit by the command of their Lord—with every matter."*— (Qur'an 97:5)

Sometimes this notion of God Manifest isn't so easy to identify, and as author Alexander Smith suggests in his book, *The Holiest Lie Ever: Glorified by Myths, Mysticism, Symbolism, Rituals and Traditions*, the symbols of the dove and fire, at times, represent the Holy Spirit. These symbols can be found in a multitude of religions, including those of the ancient Greeks, the Romans, the Druids, the Egyptians, the Incas, the Hindus, the Buddhists, and the Celts, who claim their Salic Laws were guided by Sat Guru. The Celts named The Holy Spirit, Salo Ghost. Vishnu is the name given by the Hindu religion.

Although it might appear as if there are two, God Unmanifest and Primander, there is actually only one. It's difficult to comprehend. A distinction there is and a distinction there isn't.

> *"The Guru is God, and God is the Guru, O Nanak; there is no difference between the two, O Siblings of Destiny. ||4||1||8||"*— (Sri Guru Granth Sahib Ji, ang 442 of 1430)

This said, *Sri Guru Granth Sahib Ji* clearly draws a distinction between God Manifest and God Unmanifest.

> *"O Servant of the Lord, O True Guru, O True Primal Being, I offer my prayers to You, O Guru."* — (Sri Guru Granth Sahib Ji, ang 492 of 1430)

> *"Without the True Guru, no one has obtained the Lord; without the True Guru, no one has obtained the Lord."* — (Sri Guru Granth Sahib Ji, ang 466 of 1430)

> *"O Nanak, by perfect good karma, you shall meet the True Guru, and then the Dear Lord, by His Sweet Will, shall bless you with His Mercy."* — (Sri Guru Granth Sahib Ji, ang 591 of 1430)

The Unmanifest is ONE. All are within ONE. ONE is within all. ONE is the Beginning. ONE is the End. ONE is Timeless. ONE is Formless. ONE is Limitless. ONE is Omnipotent. ONE is Omniscient. ONE is Fathomless. And ONE is the Primal Energy—everything known and unknown—differentiations from.

A common understanding there is, God is Unmanifest and God is also Spiritually-Manifest. The Great Architect is in all creation and all creation is in The Great Architect—the Unmanifest aspect. Simultaneously, God is unto the self, outside all creation, and interacts with God Unmanifest—the Spiritually-Manifest aspect.

Unfortunately, popular culture has trapped the mind to think of God inside a box and this limits a person's spiritual cognisance.

Under this narrative, when a person hears the word "God", their mind naturally brings forth the images and the associations they absorbed to represent the idea of God. It's similar to what occurs when a person hears the word "apple", and the phenomenon can limit a person's awareness and spiritual progress.

Under this narrative, "God" is confined to an image of an old man, with a white beard, floating amid the clouds, constantly wrestling the devil, and daily administering punishment. Or a young man, with dusty-blonde hair, and blue eyes. Or for that matter, a God represented by a particular colour, form, or gender.

Any attribute that limits the power of The Creator isn't truthful. God is much more and the human mind isn't powerful enough to grasp The Unfathomable. I'm not capable of giving even the smallest of the most miniscule of accounts.

Although I use different names such as God, The Father, The Great-Giver, and The Great Architect to denote ONE, please recognize that my intention isn't to limit ONE inside a box.

A person has the potential to build a relationship with God Manifest, but God Unmanifest cannot be found or understood solely by woman or man, and only Sat Guru can introduce a person to The Lord. Furthermore, God's Spirit is a teacher—the all-knowing and always truthful Professor. A lecture conducted by The Spirit will reveal reality's true nature. But only when the student is ready, will the teacher appear.

> *"For God has revealed them to us by his Spirit. The Spirit searches all things, even the deep things of God."*— (1 Corinthians 2:10)

> *"We have not received the spirit of the world but the Spirit who is from God, that we may understand what God has freely given us."*— (1 Corinthians 2:12)

All gifts worth holding rest with Sat Guru and a true religious philosophy aims to guide a person toward Salo Ghost. This by revealing the wisdom required to experience an encounter with The Truest Teacher. This Supreme Professor guided every true Holy individual.

"And Jesus, when he was baptized, went up straightway out of the water: and, lo, the heavens were opened unto him, and he saw the Spirit of God descending like a dove, and lighting upon him."— (Matthew 3:16)

To experience a visit by God's Spirit a person must correctly be, and suggestions such as the following create an invisible state of being God's Spirit favours.

- *Selfless service.*
- *Egalitarianism.*
- *Employment of the five weapons (love, truth, contentment, compassion, and humility).*
- *Selflessness.*
- *Meditation.*
- *Remembering The Source.*
- *Praising The Great Architect through song.*
- *Mantras (e.g. Mool Mantra).*
- *Saintly companionship.*

Every living thing emanates an invisible presence and God's Spirit is attracted by the presence generated by the mentioned. An individual who adheres to these suggestions emanates a favourable vibration and, if Karma permits, the person will experience a visit by The Truest Teacher. This is a natural law.

Now, what do the above suggestions truly generate? Love. To connect with God's Spirit is the goal and the means is love. Unconditionally love all, for all is ONE, and the vibration an individual generates under this influence is ideal for a celestial encounter. A persons's constitution produces a resonance Sat Guru favours. Without this presence, God Manifest doesn't reveal the self.

> *"For the sinful nature desires what is contrary to the Spirit, and the Spirit what is contrary to the sinful nature. They are in conflict with each other, so that you are not to do whatever you want."*— (Galatians 5:17)

Just as the above suggestions produce the ideal state of being, a person can also create a presence that builds a barrier between Primander and him or her. This too is a natural law and such examples as the following contaminate an individual's state of being.

- *Alcohol, nicotine, and carnivorous eating.*
- *Corrupt company and degenerate establishments.*
- *The five thieves (lust, anger, greed, ego, and attachment).*

- *Slander.*

To meet God's Spirit is the highest earthly purpose. The formula is simple but difficult to practice. Those who can are the best of the living. And God's Spirit doesn't necessarily appear to an individual. Sat Guru can speak within a person and to a person. Yet, do not confuse the inner dialogue the mind generates with instructions from The Spirit. The voice of The Truest Teacher is distinct and sounds not where the mind's dialogue unfolds.

The influence and instruction of Sat Guru is necessary to garner The Word and The Name, and to understand The Great Architect. Without this, no person will truly grasp the wonders of God. If a person were to forget all religion and entrust strictly in the Holy Spirit, they will gain enlightenment. The Holy Spirit taught all the prophets. For this reason, religions have much in common. The source was the same and the differences are earthly assertions.

The Perfect Guru teaches the person and no individual can truly understand the nature of reality without the Holy Spirit. But God's Spirit can do much more for the God seeker. Sat Guru can purify and unite.

In an instant, the Holy Spirit can transform the beliefs, thoughts, and wants of a person. This includes the neural pathways that facilitate them. The Spirit of God has the ability to bring a change to the body and mind, and this change is in harmony with the expectations of the Holy Spirit. This transformation allows the spirit to rise to become the dominant source of information influencing an individual's time and space of thought.

> *"But the fruit of the Spirit is love, joy, peace, patience, kindness, goodness, faithfulness."* — (Galatians 5:22)

A person's time and space of thought is influenced by two dominant databases of information. These two sources of information are the body and the spirit. The goal is to quiet the body's information so to allow the spirit's information to influence the time and space of thought. Only then is Jivan Mukti (salvation) an exercisable option.

The goal is to quiet the body so to allow the spirit to speak, and only The Word and The Name can permanently silence the body and release the spirit. However, no person will bask in these two sacred vibrations without Sat Guru. Only God's Spirit gifts The Word and The Name.

The true "I" is not the body. The body is only a temporary vehicle. The true "I" is the driver. Yet, without recognizing this, a person lives in cruise control, and the destination is determined by the body's programming and desires.

The first step before an individual can battle to release the spirit is to recognize that the body is not the true "I". The true "I" existed before this body and the true "I" will continue to be after the fall of the flesh.

> *"He saved us, not because of righteous things we had done, but because of his mercy. He saved us through the washing of rebirth and renewal by the Holy Spirit."*—(Titus 3:5)

The Spirit of God has the power to set right the manner in which a person operates and a purification is a requirement before an individual can unite with The Formless. Consider this. The person is like a drop of water dyed with purple color, in a body of the clearest water. Until the purple color is removed from the droplet, it will never truly merge into the whole. Sat Guru eliminates this color. Without God's Spirit, regardless of how thin the color might get, the person will never truly merge.

God Unmanifest introduces God Spiritually-Manifest to a person, and the second unites an individual with God Unmanifest. That is, after a rebirth.

An individual may have mastered their chakras, learned how to manipulate the principles of the Universe so to perform miracles, or accumulated all the wealth the planet has to offer, but without Sat Guru, they will never merge with The Great Architect. Salo Ghost is the only able to blend a person with God, and this by activating God's Word and The Name. The Word and The Name are within every individual and their nature liberates the true self and provides a link to The Eternal.

So please, love God's Spirit and love all God's creations. In God's Mercy, The Great Architect will send God's Spirit. Primander truthfully teaches and can activate the sacred frequencies within. These frequencies allow the "I" to experience the absolute reality. Through the mind of a saint, union with The Source can be achieved. A permanent love, in the truest sense, can soak through to every gene and every inch of a person's being. All is yours and the first step is to correctly be.

> *"Flesh gives birth to flesh, but the Spirit gives birth to spirit. You should not be surprised at my saying, 'You must be born again.' The wind blows wherever it pleases. You hear its sound, but you cannot tell where it comes from or where it is going. So it is with everyone born of the Spirit."*— (John 3:6-8)

THE RESURRECTION

Before I better understood the image of dead Jesus on a cross, the depiction provoked uncomfortable feelings. The symbol shows the superhuman Jesus as a defeated person. But how can this be when Jesus was under the protection of God? Nothing can penetrate The Father's Shield.

The mainstream interpretation didn't do much to quell my discomfort. If anything, it spawned more confusion. Serendipitously, I stumbled across a very old understanding. According to Manly P. Hall, the ancient adepts of the world symbolized Maya/Mammon, or the material, as a cube. An unfolded cube takes the shape of a cross.

Along this line of thought, Jesus' dead body on the cross represents the triumph of the spirit over the human body and Maya. It's the death of the material body while still living, the resurrection of the spirit, and Jesus' rebirth through it. As mentioned, this occurs by way of God's Word, and after a resurrection, the subconscious merges with an individual's conscious state and the principle element influencing this awareness is the spirit, and the commander of the spirit is The Father.

The image further depicts a fragile Jesus. This teaches us that spiritual growth includes immense suffering. Without suffering, and for an ego-centered mind, typically, the consciousness will not expand to seek and comprehend more than Mammon. Suffering breaks the egoic bubble and swells a person's awareness to validate the spiritual and the spirit. Suffering is a blessing.

The egoic bubble evolves as a person, under the dominance of the ego, interacts with the material world, and the bubble's value system is centered on the supremacy of the egoic self and Mammon. This bubble limits a person's awareness of reality—without an individual knowing it.

Suffering bursts the bubble, and unfortunately, this will likely bring about more suffering. Cognitive dissonance and depression is a natural outcome when a value system no longer holds prominence or worth. A person who then interacts with society and her members, under the influence of a shattered value system, will surely and slowly experience social and financial marginalization. The most painful side-effect will be friends and family who do not understand. The isolation and ridicule will hurt. Resource less to purchase help, many nights will be spent crying out to the Universe.

Loneliness, ridicule, and poverty, accompanied by cognitive dissonance and depression, can provoke suicidal thoughts and many dances with the shadow of Death. But hopefully, the individual experiencing the aftermath of a burst is strong enough to endure this trial by fire, and through the suffering, able to sweep away the ashes and construct a more truthful value system—one no longer centered on the egoic self and Maya.

Suffering can rupture the egoic bubble and this is the first step to conquering the body's influences and recognizing reality before and beyond the material. Suffering is a prerequisite to sainthood.

The ego is the Commander and if it can be captured, as can the army (the body's influences such as anger and greed). But once it's taken into custody, the ego and its army will torment the warden (the person attempting to evolve past the body). This too causes extreme agony. Yet, if a person can keep them imprisoned long enough, with meditation, proper thought, proper conduct, and prayer, God's Spirit will descend and permanently switch off the influences of the body—The Holy Ghost will permanently quiet the captors.

To live for more than the material and to master the body involves immense suffering. No person can truly empathize with those who've survived the fire. Only those who've also experienced the flames can. People as Jesus deserve their status. They are kings amid men and women.

In my interpretation, the symbol of dead Jesus on a cross has evolved to host a dual meaning. In this, the initial understanding represents so much more than the popular depiction and it doesn't show Jesus as a defeated person. On the contrary, Jesus is depicted as superhuman, for Jesus conquered Mammon and transformed into a Christ. The cross is a symbol of Jesus' Christhood.

Since we're discussing the symbol of the cross, I'd like to note that the cross is not exclusive to Christendom and the symbol was used for many, many millennia before the birth of Jesus. Nor is the cross a universal symbol representing one particular notion. Sometimes, it denotes the Sun. Sometimes, it represents east, west, north, and south. Sometimes, it symbolizes the number 9. Sometimes, when with a circle, it's an astrological tool. Sometimes, it symbolizes the water deities. Sometimes, it's an emblem of Heaven and immortality. And sometimes, it's associated to the Christ.

If the interpretation I present is correct, how is it that Jesus on the cross is understood differently?

Christendom experienced the European dark ages and it's possible the people of then didn't understand the cross as symbolic. From which, misinterpretations arose, and those misunderstandings are still with us today.

DEAD YET ALIVE

> *"Then Jesus said to His disciples, "If anyone desires to come after Me, let him deny himself, and take up his cross, and follow Me. For whoever desires to save his life will lose it, but whoever loses his life for My sake will find it. For what profit is it to a man if he gains the whole world, and loses his own soul? Or what will a man give in exchange for his soul?"* — (Matthew 16:24-26)

The Glorious Jesus taught his follows how to perform greater miracles than him, but this lesson is lost in translation and the truth of the matter is hidden. Luckily, the teaching can be decoded and the first step is to carry your own cross and to do as Jesus. Yet, to literally bare the cross will not gift a person salvation, and to carry the cross is to battle the body's influences and the material stimulants that love the body's programming more than the spirit's. To carry the cross is to conquer one's physical presence without actually dying.

To kill the body while still alive is to dominate the body's programming/constitution, so to allow the spirit's constitution to influence the conscious framework. The body houses units of information such as anger and sadness. These units allow a person to experience such things as anger and sadness. Without these units of information, a person will not experience anger or sadness and Thought Energy is free of these influences. This is the goal, to be free of the body's programming. When this occurs, the spirit rises.

The spirit too houses units of information, along with tools equivalent to the body's senses—they allow the consciousness to sense what the five body senses cannot. The units of the spirit produce a conscious awareness different from a Thought Energy influenced by the body's units. It is an awareness aligned with The Source.

Only those who rise above the influences of their body and free the spirit will live right. But how many people can levitate above Mammon? The impulses of the body are strong. Daily, even the smartest, the strongest, the richest, and the most influential person is overpowered by them. For this reason, the assist of Sat Guru is required.

THE SECOND DEATH

In the eyes of a spiritual adept, those who do not realize the spirit are as good as dead, while he or she still has breath. True living is living in God's Will.

True living cannot be experienced until the influences of the body are silenced and the spirit within is governing the time and space of thought. The path is narrow like the sharp edge of a sword. However, there is no other method if a person wishes to live truthfully. Until then, dead and in darkness a person is.

> *"Then they went in and did not find the body of the Lord Jesus. And it happened, as they were greatly[b] perplexed about this, that behold, two men stood by them in shining garments. Then, as they were afraid and bowed their faces to the earth, they said to them, 'Why do you seek the living among the dead? He is not here, but is risen!'"* — (Luke 24:3-6)

The New Testament speaks of two deaths and two resurrections.

> *"Blessed and holy is he that hath part in the first resurrection: on such the second death hath no power,*

> *but they shall be priests of God and of Christ, and shall reign with him a thousand years."* — (Revelation 20:6)

In my interpretation, after applying my spiritual understanding, the first death symbolizes the death of the body while a person still lives, and the second death is the release of the true self from the body. In the second death, the body is actually dead.

That individual who experiences the first death, in this life and after the body perishes, truly lives, and after the second death, which only The Source determines, he or she exist as God's favorite. But, if the first death isn't achieved, the second death will not be the highest manifestation.

If the first death is experienced, it's vital to stay the course. Jesus, up to his last moment, before his second death, in the midst of excruciating pain, didn't regress and nullify his first death.

If the theory of reincarnation is applied, then the second death, if the first death is achieved, symbolizes freedom from the cycle of life and death and a manifestation as an angelic being. However, if the first death isn't experienced, the second death will reintroduce the "I" into the cycle—the outcome determined by what a person sows—the good and the bad are calculated.

When reading specific Biblical passages, and many there are, it feels as if the writers are actually expressing the notion of reincarnation. At times, the term refers to the rebirth of the spirit and the death of the body's influences, and at other times, the word appears to represent the idea of reincarnation.

> *"Marvel not at this: for the hour is coming, in the which all that are in the graves shall hear his voice, and shall come forth; they that have done good, unto the resurrection of life; and they that have done evil, unto the resurrection of damnation."* — (John 5:28-29)

> *"But this I confess unto thee, that after the way which they call heresy, so worship I the God of my fathers, believing all things which are written in the law and in the prophets: And have hope toward God, which they themselves also allow, that there shall be a resurrection of the dead, both of the just and unjust."* — (Acts 24:14-15)

Karma is an integral cog in the machine that is reincarnation and *the Bible* often speaks of karma.

> *"Be not deceived; God is not mocked: for whatsoever a man soweth, that shall he also reap."* — (Galatians 6:7)

Karma is linked to the principles of reincarnation. One is not without the other. When a person's ascendance occurs, a person's energy, shaped by the actions in life, determines what environment that energy will gravitate towards.

The shape or make-up of a person's energy determines to where and what their energy will again manifest. Manifestation and energy attract each other. Certain types or shapes of energy naturally attract to specific manifestations. It's all cause and effect. Even demi-gods are subject.

So, karma not only plays a role in the type of daily experiences an individual encounters, karma also prescribes what type of existence a person is born to. Genetics, inherited wealth, life experiences, innate spirituality, etc., are the result of a person's past life karma.

> *"And even the very hairs of your head are all numbered."* — (Matthew 10:30)

A person's constitution is predetermined and not random, and a person is born to a specific karma. Although there might be a day-to-day deliberation, and day-to-day causes and effects, all is predetermined beforehand. A person's karma is determined by their previous existence and the karma of their future self is determined by their current state of existence. It's an equation. There is no escaping it. It's written in the cosmos and the planets know it. Regardless of how much you might think you're the author of experiences, it's actually a cognitive illusion.

This said, God scripts each living things karma, it's foreordained, and The Formless is the only able to rewrite what is written. The script can be updated, but before this can happen, the first step is to connect with God and request a revision.

Accordingly, a person is not trapped to their karma. You are not who you were and you will not be who you are. Beg The Father for perfect karma—the type that provides the foremost second death.

To one degree or another, most of the world's religions teach about reincarnation and karma—including the Jewish faith. The *Zohar* clearly details the concepts. However, in a few religious houses, the teachings aren't explicit, even though the ideas can be identified within their doctrine.

> *"So whatever you wish that others would do to you, do also to them, for this is the Law and the Prophets."* — (Matthew 7:12)

THREE DAYS

After a person is prepared, it takes three days of spiritual activity to free the time and space of thought (Thought Energy) from the influences of the body and the material realm. It takes three days to conquer the beasts. After three days, the outcome is a mystical experience. This results in the resurrection of the spirit. The spirit was free and alive before it descended into the body. The body, if enslaved to Mammon, cages the spirit. In such a state, the spirit is considered dead until it rises above its captor.

In an allegorical fashion, the following passages refer to these three days.

> *"And Joseph answered and said, 'This is the interpretation thereof: The three baskets are three days: Yet within three days shall Pharaoh lift up thy head from off thee, and shall hang thee on a tree; and the birds shall eat thy flesh from off thee.' And it came to pass the third day, which was Pharaoh's birthday, that he made a feast unto all his servants: and he lifted up the head of the chief butler and of the chief baker among his servants."* —(Genesis 40:18-20)

The Pharaoh represents the spirit.

> *"And I have said, I will bring you up out of the affliction of Egypt unto the land of the Canaanites, and the Hittites, and the Amorites, and the Perizzites, and the Hivites, and the Jebusites, unto a land flowing with milk and honey. And they shall hearken to thy voice: and thou shalt come, thou and the elders of Israel, unto the king of Egypt, and ye shall say unto him, The Lord God of the Hebrews hath met with us: and now let us go, we beseech thee, three days' journey into the wilderness, that we may sacrifice to the Lord our God. And I am sure that the king of Egypt will not let you go, no, not by a mighty hand."* — (Exodus 3:17-19)

Egypt represents the body and the body's rule over the time and space of thought. The land of milk and honey symbolizes an existence with the spirit as the captain of Thought Energy.

> *"And Pharaoh said, Who is the Lord, that I should obey his voice to let Israel go? I know not the Lord, neither will I let Israel go. And they said, The God of the Hebrews hath met with us: let us go, we pray thee, three days' journey into the desert, and sacrifice unto the Lord our God; lest he fall upon us with pestilence, or with the sword. And the king of Egypt said unto them,*

Wherefore do ye, Moses and Aaron, let the people from their works? get you unto your burdens." — (Exodus 5:2-4)

Israel symbolizes the spirit, the Pharaoh the body, and the pestilence and the sword represent extreme suffering.

"...for we shall sacrifice the abomination of the Egyptians to the Lord our God: lo, shall we sacrifice the abomination of the Egyptians before their eyes, and will they not stone us? We will go three days' journey into the wilderness, and sacrifice to the Lord our God, as he shall command us. And Pharaoh said, I will let you go, that ye may sacrifice to the Lord your God in the wilderness; only ye shall not go very far away: intreat for me." — (Exodus 8:26-28)

The Egyptians represent the body's influences. The wilderness represents an environment unwelcoming to the body.

"And Moses stretched forth his hand toward heaven; and there was a thick darkness in all the land of Egypt three days: They saw not one another, neither rose any from his place for three days: but all the children of Israel had light in their dwellings. And Pharaoh called

unto Moses, and said, Go ye, serve the Lord; only let your flocks and your herds be stayed: let your little ones also go with you." — (Exodus 10:22-24)

The three days of darkness in the land of Egypt equates to three days of ignoring Maya.

"And it shall be, if thou go with us, yea, it shall be, that what goodness the Lord shall do unto us, the same will we do unto thee. And they departed from the mount of the Lord three days' journey: and the ark of the covenant of the Lord went before them in the three days' journey, to search out a resting place for them. And the cloud of the Lord was upon them by day, when they went out of the camp." — (Numbers 10:32-34)

In these three days, The Father will be a guide.

"Then Joshua commanded the officers of the people, saying, Pass through the host, and command the people, saying, Prepare you victuals; for within three days ye shall pass over this Jordan, to go in to possess the land, which the Lord your God giveth you to possess it." — (Joshua 1:10-11)

The land represents the body, and it takes three days of specific spiritual practice to become complete master over the body.

> *"And it came to pass after three days, that the officers went through the host; And they commanded the people, saying, When ye see the ark of the covenant of the Lord your God, and the priests the Levites bearing it, then ye shall remove from your place, and go after it."* — (Joshua 3:2-3)

In this passage, the Ark of the Covenant represents a spiritual guide, or a spiritual marker, or possibly The Holy Ghost, who appears after three days.

> *"Now the Lord had prepared a great fish to swallow up Jonah. And Jonah was in the belly of the fish three days and three nights."* — (Jonah 1:17)

Jonah in the belly represents three days of isolation.

> *"For as Jonas was three days and three nights in the whale's belly; so shall the Son of man be three days and three nights in the heart of the earth. The men of Nineveh shall rise in judgment with this generation, and shall condemn it: because they repented at the*

> *preaching of Jonas; and, behold, a greater than Jonas is here."* — (Matthew 12:40-41)

> *"And he charged them that they should tell no man of him. And he began to teach them, that the Son of man must suffer many things, and be rejected of the elders, and of the chief priests, and scribes, and be killed, and after three days rise again."* — (Mark 8:30-31)

Three days of specific spiritual activity and a person will rise after which. In these three days, a person will experience immense suffering.

> *"And there arose certain, and bare false witness against him, saying, We heard him say, I will destroy this temple that is made with hands, and within three days I will build another made without hands."* — (Mark 14:57-59)

Three days of specific spiritual activity are required to conquer the influences of the body.

> *"And Saul arose from the earth; and when his eyes were opened, he saw no man: but they led him by the hand, and brought him into Damascus. And he was*

three days without sight, and neither did eat nor drink. And there was a certain disciple at Damascus, named Ananias; and to him said the Lord in a vision, Ananias. And he said, Behold, I am here, Lord." — (Acts 9:8-10)

"And their dead bodies shall lie in the street of the great city, which spiritually is called Sodom and Egypt, where also our Lord was crucified. And they of the people and kindreds and tongues and nations shall see their dead bodies three days and an half, and shall not suffer their dead bodies to be put in graves. And they that dwell upon the earth shall rejoice over them, and make merry, and shall send gifts one to another; because these two prophets tormented them that dwelt on the earth." — (Revelation 11:8-10)

Three days after a person is prepared. Three days of suffering. Three days before a rebirth.

The story of Jesus' burial and resurrection too expresses a three-day spiritual journey. After a person is prepared to embrace the three days, at the end of three days, their body's influences will permanently quiet and the spirit will surge and influence Thought Energy. This is the true meaning of a rebirth.

> *"And that he was buried, and that he rose again the third day according to the scriptures..."* — (1 Corinthians 15:4)

Other stories also exist that include a three-day event, a death, and a resurrection. For example, in the story of the Masonic Grand Master Hiram Abiff, the Grand Master resurrects after three days (with some accounts suggested that he rose after fifteen days). He was known to hold the Sacred Word.

In the story of Guru Nanak, there too is a three-day journey. It is said that he was underwater, and lost, for three days before he re-emerged as a Christ. I'm sure if we look closely at the stories of the other spiritual masters, we'll find a three-day parable.

MOOL MANTRA

The following prayer/mantra was written by Guru Nanak and inspired by God's Spirit. This mantra is a brief description of God, and simultaneously, it reveals the nature of the cosmos.

Ik Onkar. Sat Naam. Kartaa Purakh. Nirbhau. Nirvair. Akaal Moorat. Ajooni Saibhang. Gurprasad.

> *"Ik: There is ONE (Ik) reality, the origin and the source of everything. The creation did not come out of nothing. When there was nothing, there was ONE, Ik.*
>
> *Onkar: When Ik becomes the creative principal it becomes Onkar. Onkar manifests as visible and invisible phenomenon. The creative principle is not separated from the created—it is present throughout the creation in an unbroken form, 'kaar'.*
>
> *Sat Naam: The sustaining principle of Ik is Sat Naam, the True Name.*
>
> *Kartaa Purakh: Ik Onkar is Creator (Purakh) and Doer (Kartaa) of everything.*

Nirbhau: That Ik Onkar is devoid of any fear, because there is nothing but itself.

Nirvair: That Ik Onkar is devoid of any enmity, because there is nothing but itself.

Akaal Moorat: That Ik Onkar is beyond Time (Akaal) and yet existing.

Ajooni: That Ik Onkar does not condense and come into any birth. All the phenomenon of birth and death of forms are within it.

Saibhang: That Ik Onkar exists on its own, by its own. It is not caused by anything before it or beyond it.

Gurprasaad: That Ik Onkar expresses itself through God-Manifest, known as Sat Guru. Through the Lord's grace and mercy (Prasaad) this happens."

(Source: http://www.sikhiwiki.org/index.php/Mool_Mantar)

The above Mool Mantra is the popular version, and several people believe, including myself, that the following was initially the ending of this mantra. I support this position simply because without the following additions, the mantra feels incomplete and abruptly ends.

Jap. Aad sach. Jugaad sach. Hai bhee sach. Nanak hose bhee sach.

> *Jap: Chant*
> *Aad sach: True in the Primal Beginning.*
> *Jugaad sach: True throughout the different epochs.*
> *Hai bhee sach: True here and now.*
> *Nanak hosee bhee sach: Forever true, says Nanak.*

This mantra is extremely powerful and all mantras, prayers, or music written by a truly holy person, through whom God speaks, are so because the holy individual combined specific sounds together to make celestial sentences and these sounds power-up a person's magnetic field and the surrounding environments. A strong magnetic field is the key to a good life.

> *By thinking, He cannot be reduced to thought, even by thinking hundreds of thousands of times."* — (Sri Guru Granth Sahib Ji, ang 1 of 1430)

ALL IS WITHIN

The Eternal Commander and Chief created all, and in doing so, The Eternal infused The Essence that is God within everything that exists. Without this Essence, there would be nothing to support the Universe and all its principles and inhabitants, including the human condition's breath of life. For this reason, every single human being is equal to another.

This idea of God within the individual troubles some religious institutions, and I think it's because they don't fully understand the notion. It seems as if the belief of God within the human condition implies to some that the person is God. However, this isn't the case. God is within all creation and separate from (onto Thyself).

Not surprisingly, in the beginning, the above notion wasn't foreign. However, particular rulers didn't like the idea. Such ideas might discourage the people from invading other people's places, taking their possessions, murdering them, and stealing their land to expand a ruler's interests. To hurt another is to hurt the God within them, and why would any person who appreciates the idea endeavour to hurt another knowing The Primal Void also feels it?

"Jesus said, 'If they say to you -where did you come from? Say to them—we came from the light, the place where the light came into being on its own accord and established [itself] and became manifest through their image. If they say to you—is it you? Say—we are its children, we are the elect of the Living Father. If they ask you—what is the sign of your father in you? Say to them—it is movement and repose.'" — (Gospel of Thomas)

Countless saints have spoken of God in such a manner. Great philosophers such as Aristotle and Pythagoras too expressed the idea. The All-Mind is within all minds.

They further suggested that to discover The Light within (God's Essence) is the highest life purpose.

The purpose is to allow The Light (God) within to govern the mind and body so to eventually merge with The Supreme Light. When The Light within is discovered, nurtured, and finally merged with The Supreme Light, an individual is considered one with The Primal Void and The Primal Void is considered one with the individual. If an individual does reach this state of being, there is little difference between the two. Moreover, he or she is no longer subject to the principles of the Universe that govern life and death.

The potential for immortality is the individual's but not immortality of the physical. Death can be overcome.

So, search for The Light within, God is closer to you than some popular religions have propagated. As Jesus expressed, the true church is within the body fortress.

> *"Neither shall they say, Lo here! or, lo there! for, behold, the kingdom of God is within you."* — (Luke 17:21)

God is within and there's a concentration of the God Essence within the heart and the heart chakra. The Egyptians believed so strongly in this idea that when they mummified a dead body, they would throw away the brain and pay overwhelming attention to the heart. The heart was more valuable than the brain.

The Egyptians were not and are not the only people who give the heart and the heart chakra importance. Most other spiritual paths that utilize the chakras of the human condition also accommodate the same understanding.

> *"Wherever I look, I see that One Lord alone. Deep within each and every heart, He Himself is contained.*

||*1*||*Pause*||" — (Sri Guru Granth Sahib Ji, ang 387 of 1430)

If you can, listen to the heart and think from the heart—allow the information within the heart chakra to influence the time and space of thought.

The Eternal Commander and Chief created all, and in doing so, The Eternal infused the Essence that is God within everything that exists. Without this Essence, there would be nothing to support the Universe and all her principles and inhabitants.

....

The popular religions believe that all creation sprung from God's Word, God's Breath, or God separated Thy Self. They all claim that creation came from a singular point. If this is true, then nothing within the Universe is without elements from this singular point of creation. Thus, God must also be within. But please don't be mistaken, there is only ONE.

HOW THE MASTER ANSWERS

> *"The True Guru is the All-knowing Primal Being; He shows us our true home within the home of the self. The Panch Shabad, the Five Primal Sounds, resonate and resound within; the insignia of the Shabad is revealed there, vibrating gloriously."* — (Sri Guru Granth Sahib Ji, ang 1291 of 1430)

Ask Sat Guru and you will receive an answer.

The distance between you and a direct answer depends on the cleanliness of your magnetic field. The cleaner and stronger a person's invisible presence, the more direct the answer.

A dirty and weak metaphysical presence welcomes indirect and obscure answers, and for an untrained mind, it will be difficult to identify this type of response. The answer might briefly flash before an individual, and in the form of a sentence deep within a book. Or the answer might reveal itself through another person and the notions he or she is sharing. Or the answer might be illustrated through the behaviour of birds. The list of indirect methods of delivering an answer is unending and God's Spirit can orchestrate any invisible and visible thing within the Universe to convey a reply.

Those individuals with a clean and strong invisible presence receive direct answers and the most direct answer manifests as an inner whisper. God's Spirit can speak to a person, and from within, a person will hear.

My friend, do your best to garner and maintain a superior aura. If you can achieve this, anything you wish to know can be known, and it will be a matter of asking the right question.

"Even if the mortal could reduce himself to the size of an atom, and through the ethers, worlds and realms, shoot in the blink of an eye, O Nanak, without the Holy Saint, he shall not be saved. ||2||"— (Sri Guru Granth Sahib Ji, ang 1360 of 1430)

HOLY COMPANIONS

Sri Guru Granth Sahib firmly believes that meditation on or contemplation of The Name and The Word have greater spiritual merit than any visit to a sacred place of pilgrimage, material object, prayer, posture, or Holy Book. The most exalted offering a person can make to The Eternal is The Name and The Word.

Meditation on or contemplation of The Name and The Word is important and not just solitary reflection. The practice, within a society of saints (Saadh Sangat or Sat Sangat), is highly valued by *Sri Guru Granth Sahib*. If you ever, by God's Grace, encounter a true society of saints, take the time to meditate with them. If you can, selflessly serve them. A true saint is immersed in The Name and The Word, and openly vibrates them. In such a state of being, their identical-self has consumed the self and there is little difference between him or her and The Great Architect. Tell me—is there any earthly person more worthy of selfless service?

> *"In the Saadh Sangat, the Company of the Holy, the Lord of the World is understood."* —(Sri Guru Granth Sahib Ji, ang 1156 of 1430))

The notion that there is very little difference, if any, between God and those saints who've merged with The Lord isn't exclusive to the Sikh doctrine and I've encountered this idea in almost all the religions I studied. Even in *the New Testament* the idea is found. Yet, please remember, although a person might merge with The Lord, the person is still of The Lord.

> *(Jesus said) "And he that seeth me seeth him that sent me."* — (John 12:45)

> *(Jesus said) "I and my Father are one."* — (John 10:30)

> *(Jesus said) "Don't you believe that I am in the Father, and that the Father is in me? The words I say to you I do not speak on my own authority. Rather, it is the Father, living in me, who is doing his work."* — (John 14:10)

In this respect, Guru Nanak and others too were The Father. Guru Nanak and others too merged with The ONE.

The true saints are above the duality of the mind—they are egoless and absorbed in The Name and The Word. For them, the world exists, and by their angelic efforts, such as celestial meditation, the world continues to exist. If God has favourites, they are it, and amid them, Sat Guru is. If you wish to find the Holy Spirit, one method is to search out a society of saints. In the Saadh Sangat, Primander plays.

> *"The Treasure of the Naam, the Name of the Lord, is found in the Saadh Sangat, the Company of the Holy."* — (Sri Guru Granth Sahib Ji, ang 1300 of 1430))

> *"The Saadh Sangat, the Company of the Holy, is heaven itself. ||4||8||16||"* — (Sri Guru Granth Sahib Ji, ang 1161 of 1430))

In this day and age, it's difficult to locate a true society of saints. Nevertheless, group prayer and meditation is still valuable. Moreover, in a group, sing the Lord's praise. As spoken of by *Guru Granth Sahib Ji*, the benefits of Kirtan (singing the Lord's praise) are:

> *"When the Saints became kind and compassionate, they told me this. Understand, that whoever sings the Kirtan of God's Praises, has performed all religious rituals. || 2 ||"* — (Sri Guru Granth Sahib Ji, ang 902 of 1430))

> *"The Lord's servant sings the Kirtan of His Praises as his worship, deep meditation, self-discipline and*

religious observances."— (Sri Guru Granth Sahib Ji, ang 498 of 1430))

"Sing the Kirtan, the Praises of the Lord, the Giver of peace, the Destroyer of pain; He shall bless you with perfect spiritual wisdom. Sexual desire, anger and greed shall be shattered and destroyed, and your foolish ego will be dispelled." — (Sri Guru Granth Sahib Ji, ang 979 of 1430)

"Your humble servant, who obtains the Medicine of the Naam, is rid of the illnesses of countless lifetimes and incarnations. So sing the Kirtan of the Lord's Praises, day and night. This is the most fruitful occupation." — (Sri Guru Granth Sahib Ji, ang 107-108 of 1430)

Kirtan has many benefits, and along with the mentioned, the sounds and vibrations created by the type of kirtan prescribed by *Guru Granth Sahib Ji* strengthens a person's magnetic field.

Every person, thing, and place emanates a magnetic field, or what some might call an aura, and a person's magnetic field influences his or her thoughts, actions, health, luck, and the type of experiences an individual will attract. The stronger a person's aura, the better. Moreover, the higher degree of positivity he or she will encounter, and less outside influences will impact the subtle nature of an individual.

A human being has two natures, the physical and the subtle, and the latter can be influenced by sounds and vibrations. Since the physical and the subtle are interrelated, a change in the invisible component of a person naturally influences the physical half of a human. Using a candle flame, Swami Murugesu's *Flame Experiment* demonstrated the impact of certain sounds on the subtle and the material. Given specific sounds, the color of the flame would change, and as would its overall presence.

Everything in existence was first a metaphysical thing, spirit, then the physical dimension evolved from it, and all material things exist within the parameters of their subtle essence. The mystics of the world, past and present, are able to perceive the invisible nature of existence, and they can also influence this essence. If a mystic wishes to influence a material thing, he or she first manipulates the subtle essence. The invisible component to everything that exists rests in what some call the Astral Plane. This plane of existence occupies the same space as the material. If a mystic desires to, for example, heal a sick person, he or she will enter the Astral Plane and repair the subtle nature of a person, so to heal their physical component.

A strong magnetic field is key to a happy and healthy life and each person can strengthen their aura. A person can strengthen their field by vibrating correctly and this can be done through selfless service, restraint of the senses, contemplation/meditation on The Source, true prayer, celestial song, and unconditional love.

THE FOUR AGES

There are certain notions that must be acknowledged so to understand your place within this world, and one idea is that of the four ages. The post-flood ancient Egyptians, Hopis, Indians, Greeks, Mayans, and Romans all valued this idea of the four epochs, with Greek philosophy hosting an additional age, the Age of Heroes. The Indians named each era a Yug (Yuga), the Hopis used the word, World, and the Mayans labelled each epoch a Sun.

The ancient people of the world believed that the solar system continuously cycles through four ages. Each era produces a different type of civilization, as determined by the distance between humanity and God. In the first age, the people are closest to God and there exists only one religion. All people have God knowledge and all people are wardens of a God-Consciousness. However, with each proceeding age, the people regress and move further from God, God knowledge, and a God-Consciousness.

The fourth epoch is said to be the darkest of all and furthest from the era of perfect existence. It's a time of dark influences and home to untruths. To one degree or another, almost all institutions facilitate falsehoods. This includes the culture and the intelligence filled and shaped by these institutions, and every person who makes contact with them. Furthermore, the Universe is predisposed to sway a person's consciousness to favour the beast within the person over the angelic. The fourth age is the era humanity is currently in.

The four ages are as follows. The Golden Age of Sat Yuga, the Silver Age of Trayta Yuga (Ram descended in this era), the Brass Age of Dwaapar Yuga (Krishna descended in this era), and the Iron Age of Kali Yuga (also called the Age of Darkness).

> *"In the Golden Age of Sat Yuga, everyone embodied contentment and meditation; religion stood upon four feet. With mind and body, they sang of the Lord, and attained supreme peace. In their hearts was the spiritual wisdom of the Lord's Glorious Virtues. Their wealth was the spiritual wisdom of the Lord's Glorious Virtues; the Lord was their success, and to live as Gurmukh was their glory. Inwardly and outwardly, they saw only the One Lord God; for them there was no other second. They centered their consciousness lovingly on the Lord, Har, Har. The Lord's Name was their companion, and in the Court of the Lord, they obtained honor. In the Golden Age of Sat Yuga, everyone embodied contentment and meditation; religion stood upon four feet. || 1 || Then came the Silver Age of Trayta Yuga; men's minds were ruled by*

power, and they practiced celibacy and self-discipline. The fourth foot of religion dropped off, and three remained. Their hearts and minds were inflamed with anger. Their hearts and minds were filled with the horribly poisonous essence of anger. The kings fought their wars and obtained only pain. Their minds were afflicted with the illness of egotism, and their self-conceit and arrogance increased. If my Lord, Har, Har, shows His Mercy, my Lord and Master eradicates the poison by the Guru's Teachings and the Lord's Name. Then came the Silver Age of Trayta Yuga; men's minds were ruled by power, and they practiced celibacy and self-discipline. || 2 || The Brass Age of Dwaapar Yuga came, and people wandered in doubt. The Lord created the Gopis and Krishna. The penitents practiced penance, they offered sacred feasts and charity, and performed many rituals and religious rites. They performed many rituals and religious rites; two legs of religion dropped away, and only two legs remained. So many heroes waged great wars; in their egos they were ruined, and they ruined others as well. The Lord, Compassionate to the poor, led them to meet the Holy Guru. Meeting the True Guru, their filth is washed away. The Brass Age of Dwaapar Yuga came, and the people wandered in doubt. The Lord created the Gopis and Krishna. || 3 || The Lord ushered in the Dark Age, the Iron Age of Kali Yuga; three legs of religion were lost, and only the fourth leg remained intact. Acting in accordance with the Word of the Guru's Shabad, the medicine of the Lord's Name is obtained. Singing the Kirtan of the Lord's Praises, divine peace is obtained. The season of singing the Lord's Praise has arrived; the Lord's Name is glorified, and the Name of the Lord, Har, Har, grows in the field of the body. In the Dark Age of Kali Yuga, if one plants any other seed than the Name, all profit and capital is lost. Servant Nanak has found the Perfect Guru, who has revealed to him the Naam within his heart and mind. The Lord ushered in the Dark Age, the Iron Age of Kali Yuga; three legs of religion were lost, and only the fourth leg remained intact. || 4 || 4 || 11 ||"— (Sri Guru Granth Sahib Ji, ang 445-446 of 1430)

The term "Guru" used in the above passage refers to God's Spirit and not a person. The name "Har, Har" is a name used to denote God. The Sikh Holy Text employs many different names to reference God.

In the ages prior, not only are people more God oriented, with the highest orientation during the Golden Age, men and women lived longer, people were in tune with their psychic abilities, nature wasn't so alien, a greater variety of intelligent life roamed the planet, and the Earth was more giving.

There are a few theories to how long each epoch will last. Some suggest 100 000s of years. In specific, certain schools believe that the Golden Age lasts for 1 728 000 years, the Silver for 1 296 000 years, the Bronze for 864 000 years, and the Dark lasts 432 000 years. Others suggest a Cosmic Year—about 26 000 Earth years.

To what happens next, there are two theories. One suggests that the cycle starts again with Sat Yuga. Another theory suggests that the cycle doesn't begin again with Sat Yuga but instead descends after Kali Yuga passes.

It should be mentioned that before the introduction of each of the four eras, and before an age begins a decline, there happens a large-scale catastrophic event such as a deluge that erases the majority of a civilization (people, culture, architecture, knowledge, technology, etc.). Catastrophic world events take place before the introduction of an era to wipe clear what is. Each era gives birth to a new type of civilization, and for the new to fully be, in this case, the old must be near-erased. The Mayans believed that human civilizations were wiped-out five times already. The Sikh book, *Dasam Granth,* suggests approximately 21-22 times. In the Sikh accounts, at the end of each epoch, The Holy Spirit incarnates and assists humanity through the transition to the upcoming aeon. This includes re-establishing civilization. Two or three incarnations were in female form. It isn't aliens who stimulate the evolution of civilization, as suggested by the Ancient Alien Theorists, God's Spirit does. Ancient Alien Theorists do present facts but draw far-fetched associations and fail to appreciate what the ancient people recorded as their history. The human being, with the help of Heaven, is responsible for the greatness. Ancient Alien Theorists do more to misdirect than reveal the mysteries of our forgotten past.

At the end of each age, there also happens a grand battle, between what's considered good and what's considered evil. All the notable kings and their armies typically assemble. In the previous epoch, as recorded in *the Mahabharata*, the longest epic-poem—longer and greater than *the Iliad*—God's Spirit incarnated as Krishna. Krishna assisted the side considered good. *The Ramayana,* another epic tale originating from the now dead Indus Valley civilization (Punjab), describes the monstrous battle that ushered in the Bronze Age. At that time, The Holy Ghost incarnated as Ram.

> *"For I know that my redeemer liveth, and that he shall stand at the latter day upon the earth:"* — (Job 19:25)

Accordingly, the coming Redeemer has come before and never truly left. At the end of this epoch, the Redeemer, God's Spirit, will manifest and assist. As suggested by the following passage, the Redeemer will take form at Sambhala village, at the end of this epoch.

"Sambhala-grama-mukhyasya. Brahmanasya mahatmanah. Bhavane visnuyasasah. Kalkih pradurbhavisyati." — (Srimad Bhagavtam, Canto 12, chapter 2, Text 18)

Padma Purana (6.242.8-12) further suggests that this village will emerge from the interior of the earth.

With respect to this age, cultures from around the world claim that their ancestors experienced civilization-destroying deluges. Science also suggests that the world has experienced multiple large-scale floods. Fortunately, even though civilizations were annihilated, pockets of people survived their respective deluge.

After learning of the many floods the world has experienced, I'm inclined to believe that Noah and his family were one of these pockets. But this idea of Noah and his family as the only survivors is a political injection.

For example, the Sumer story of Ziusudra, the Indian story of Manu, the Greek story of Deucalion, and the Babylonian story of Utnapishtim all describe a man, who inspired by Heaven, built a boat so to survive a forthcoming flood. Some stories also detail a sea vessel capable of holding vast numbers of life. You might be inclined to think that all the tales are referring to one event and the same people, but the characteristics of each story are different from the next. There were multiple survivors besides Noah and his family.

The idea, as with others, is presented as such, with Noah's family as the sole survivors, so to persuade people that the religion Noah's story stems from is associated with the only people in the world who were permitted to live by God. The idea is designed to manipulate the patron to believe those not of their house are inferior and false. Unfortunately, enough generations have recycled the lie that now a falsehood is taken as absolute and above rational discussion.

The Mayan deluge story, and the depiction of the pre-flood world, reveals a fascinating notion that's also found in Christendom. The sacred book of the Maya, *the Popol Vuh,* tells a story of a devastating flood in which the first beings were destroyed. The Mayans and many other ancient cultures from around the world, such as the Vedic culture, suggest that in the distant past the demi-gods experimented and modified creatures. The first several creations were of an inferior character and eliminated—possibly by flood. It's said that almost all the giants of old were also lost to the oceans.

Apparently, the post-flood cultures possessed detailed and accurate world maps before the transition to the current age. The Pieri Reese Map, the Merkator Map, and the Arontios Phenious Map are said to be copies of these ancient maps. Surprisingly, these maps show no ice covering Antarctica and the topography is accurately recorded.

In each age, the alignment of the planets is different from the others and it's the change in the arrangement of the planets that stimulates catastrophic world events. In the Age of Sat Yug, in relation to the Earth, Venus and Saturn play a much more dominant role. The symbol of Islam possibly reflects this idea. Supposedly, the symbol is not of the Moon and Sun, but of Venus and Saturn. Islam is remembering a time of perfect existence.

The New Testament too expresses the idea of ages, but according to Erich von Däniken, the notion is lost in translation and the following passage is plausibly inaccurate.

> *"Teaching them to observe all things whatsoever I have commanded you: and, lo, I am with you always, even unto the end of the world. Amen."*— (Matthew 28:20)

The word, world, in the above passage is mistranslated. If correctly converted from Greek to English, the word would be "aeon". So, the passage should read:

> *"Teaching them to observe all things whatsoever I have commanded you: and, lo, I am with you always, even unto the end of the aeon. Amen."*— (Matthew 28:20)

The end of this epoch isn't the end of human existence or the end of the planet—the End-of-Days. It's only the end of this type of human living and being. The popular Christian understanding is placed within one era, this age, and not within the four. The fashionable interpretation isn't complete but presented as whole.

The parable of the statue composed of gold, silver, bronze, iron, and clay, seen by Nebuchadnezzar in his dream (*Daniel 2: 31-45*), too describes this cosmic cycle. The fifth element, the clay, references the grand cycle the four ages are contained within. The cycle of the four ages eventually ends and then is re-established. There are cycles within cycles and all cycles come to an eventual end. Yet, only to start again. God retracts creation and then, once again, expands creation.

> *"This image's head was of fine gold, his breast and his arms of silver, his belly and his thighs of brass, his legs of iron, his feet part of iron and part of clay."* — (Daniel 2: 32-33)

Interestingly, the theory of the four ages provides an answer to a question mainstream historians are troubled by. They don't know or don't believe how the early civilizations, such as the Egyptians, gained the knowledge that allowed them to spontaneously civilize. Some historians have gone as far as to suggest that aliens were responsible for their advancement. But according to the ancient Egyptians, the knowledge required to civilize came from the previous ages, and it was knowledge that survived the transition from one era to another. The Sphinx is said to be from the previous age. Geologists have determined that the Sphinx is actually older than 10 000 years. They've determined this by examining the weathering the Sphinx has experienced. The examination determined that at one point, the Sphinx was exposed to rain, and the Sahara hasn't experienced a rainfall in over 10 000 years. If this is true, then the civilizations of this age are not as advanced as the civilizations of the past. We're playing catch-up.

The supposition reminds me of a particular idea found in the Christian doctrine:

> *"What has been is what will be, and what has been done is what will be done; there is nothing new under the sun."*— (Ecclesiastes 1:4-11)

Other mysteries are also put into perspective when the theory of the four ages is applied to them. For example, the questions surrounding some of the megalithic structures found all over the world become less when considering the eras. It's possible that they were designed the sizes they were, in a previous age, to survive catastrophic world events brought forth by the transition from one epoch to another. Perhaps, Heaven inspired as Heaven motivated Noah, but instead of a boat, instructions were provided to build huge stone structures.

Whereas ships such as Noah's stored life, the megalithic structures of the world might be designed to give knowledge. They must be looked at in the right light. For example, they give accurate astrological readings, their proportions are precise and mathematically arranged, they exhibit signs that advanced technology was used to make them, and they're built on what the Chinese call dragon lines (earth energy lines). It's also possible that they were designed to store written knowledge in the form of books and such, and that knowledge was retrieved after a catastrophic event. Perhaps a storehouse of knowledge is yet to be recovered.

Ships and megalithic buildings are not the only type of structures supposedly inspired by Heaven to survive an upcoming natural disaster. For example, in the second chapter of the *Vendidad*, a division of the Zoroastrian holy book *Avesta,* God warned the Persian King Yima, the son of Vivanghat, of an upcoming natural disaster. God further instructed him to build underground cities and take shelter. Derinkuyu, the massive underground city discovered in Turkey, which can house as many as twenty thousand people and the required livestock, is said to be one of the cities Yima built.

Elaborate underground cities, complexes, and tunnel systems are not all that strange. The ancient cultures from all over the world have one story or another detailing such things. For example, the Hopi and the Apache Indians believe that their ancestors once lived underground, and only after a great calamity, did they resurface.

In his book, *Weird America*, Jim Brandon shares the legend of the city underneath California's Death Valley called "Shin-Au-Av". The story originates from the Paiute Indians, and supposedly, in this mysterious underground complex, once lived an unknown race of people. The Sioux Indians also share an underground city story, in which one of their people, White Horse, accidentally found an underground city occupied by strange humans. These underground humans gave White Horse a mystical talisman capable of melting rocks.

There are numerous stories from all over the world detailing the existence of underground cities, complexes, and tunnels. The two most famous hidden underground cities are Agharta and Shambhala.

The ancient people of the world believed that the solar system continuously cycles through four eras and humanity is currently in the fourth. In this age, only The Name and The Word will save.

IN THE BEGINNING...

> *"The same was in the beginning with God. All things were made by him; and without him was not any thing made that was made. In him was life; and the life was the light of men. And the light shineth in darkness; and the darkness comprehended it not."* — (John 1:2-5)

In the Beginning, the Heavenly darkness was, and The Spirit and The Name, together, repelled the dark. After the darkness retreated, what remained was a celestial watery essence. The Spirit then moved over the watery essence and initiated creation.

The most philosophical manuscript coveted by the ancient Egyptians was *The Primander*. This book relates a conversation between Thoth and Primander, the Supreme Intelligence. Of creation, Thoth communicates the following:

> *"I had then before my eyes a most prodigious spectacle. All things had resolved themselves into light. A marvellous, pleasing and seducing sight it was to contemplate. It filled me with delight. After a while a horrid shadow, which ended in oblique folds, and assumed a humid nature, agitated itself with terrific noise. From it escaped smoke with uproar, and a voice*

was heard above the din. It seemed as the voice of the light; and the verb came forth from that voice of light; that verb was carried upon the humid principle. Out of it came forth the fire pure and light, and rising, it was lost in the air that, spirit-like, occupies the intermediate space between the water and the fire. The earth and the water were so mixed that the surface of the Earth covered by the water appeared nowhere." — (Sacred Mysteries, Among the Mayas and the Quiches. 11, 500 Years Ago. By Augustus Le Plongeon, 1886).

The sacred book of the Quiches, *Popol-Vuh,* conveys the following:

"This is the recital of how everything was without life, calm and silent, all was motionless and quiet; void was the immensity of the heavens; the face of the Earth did not manifest itself yet; only the tranquil sea was, and the space of the heavens. All was immobility and silence in the darkness..." — (Sacred Mysteries, Among the Mayas and the Quiches. 11, 500 Years Ago. By Augustus Le Plongeon, 1886).

The *Manava-dharma-sastra,* a Vedic manuscript, suggests that:

> *"the visible universe in the beginning was nothing but darkness. Then the great, self-existing Power dispelled that darkness, and appeared in all His splendor. He first produced the waters; and on them moved Narayana the divine spirit."* — (Sacred Mysteries, Among the Mayas and the Quiches. 11, 500 Years Ago. By Augustus Le Plongeon, 1886).

The New Testament too contains a similar story.

> *"In the beginning the Earth was without form and void; and darkness was upon the face of the deep, and the spirit of God moved upon the face of the water. And God said, Let there be light and there was light."* — (Sacred Mysteries, Among the Mayas and the Quiches. 11, 500 Years Ago. By Augustus Le Plongeon, 1886).

The story of Isis, Osiris, and Set suggests that The Spirit and The Name together repel the Heavenly darkness (Set). The story also implies that when The Spirit and The Name retract, Set will again reign.

BOOKS BY MIKE BHANGU

www.ingramcontent.com/pod-product-compliance
Lightning Source LLC
Chambersburg PA
CBHW070759020526
44118CB00036B/2081